Copyright © 2018 by Cilvia Osborne

All rights reserved. No part of this publication may be reproduced, distributed or transmitted in any form or by any means, including photocopying, recording, or other electronic or mechanical methods, without the prior written permission of the publisher and author, except in the case of brief quotations embodied in critical reviews and certain other noncommercial uses permitted by copyright law. For permission requests, write to the publisher, from the contact page at the web address below.

DR. NES INTERNATIONAL
Los Angeles, CA
www.drnesintl.com

Ordering Information:
Quantity sales. Special discounts are available on quantity purchases by corporations, churches, associations, and others. For details, contact the Dr. Nes International at the above website.

You Are/Cilvia Osborne. -- 1st ed.
Illustrator: Glecia Tatum

ISBN 13: 9780999178546

Dedication

This book is dedicated to my six-year-old son, Deon Osborne. Deon, you are an inspiration and were the inspiration for this book. God gave me you and slowly downloaded what I needed to impart in you and now the world. We started with, You Are Bold, You Are Confident, You Are Smart, You Are Handsome. You started making these declarations at the age of three. Now God wants other boys and girls to begin declaring who they are as well.

Who knew, 3 years later, YOU ARE would be distributed to the world for us all to share in speaking well over ourselves intentionally and faithfully.

THANK YOU, Deon, for teaching me each day to be better than the day before.

I LOVE YOU!!

Your MOMMY!

[any blank pages are intentional]

*Note for children: Remember, only the first word in a sentence is capitalized. In this book, I didn't follow that rule. So, it's okay just for this time! ☺

YOU ARE BEAUTIFUL

Say out Loud: <u>I AM BEAUTIFUL</u>

Write It:

I AM BEAUTIFUL

DAY 2

YOU ARE CONFIDENT

Say out Loud: <u>I AM CONFIDENT</u>

Write It:

<u>I AM CONFIDENT</u>

DAY 3

YOU ARE GIFTED

Say out Loud: <u>I AM GIFTED</u>

Write It:

I AM GIFTED

DAY 4

YOU ARE RESPONSIBLE

Say out Loud: <u>I AM RESPONSIBLE</u>

Write It:

<u>I AM RESPONSIBLE</u>

DAY 5

YOU ARE COURAGEOUS

Say out Loud: I AM COURAGEOUS

Write It:

I AM COURAGEOUS

DAY 6

YOU ARE TRUSTWORTHY

Say out Loud: I AM TRUSTWORTHY

Write It:

I AM TRUSTWORTHY

DAY 7

YOU ARE POWERFUL

Say out Loud: I AM POWERFUL

Write It:

I AM POWERFUL

DAY 8

YOU ARE INSPIRING

Say out Loud: <u>I AM INSPIRING</u>

Write It:

<u>I AM INSPIRING</u>

DAY 9

YOU ARE CREATIVE

Say out Loud: <u>I AM CREATIVE</u>

Write It:

<u>I AM CREATIVE</u>

DAY 10

YOU ARE AMAZING

Say out Loud: <u>I AM AMAZING</u>

Write It:

I AM AMAZING

DAY 11

YOU ARE LOVING

Say out loud: <u>I AM LOVING</u>

Write It:

I AM LOVING

DAY 12

YOU ARE DRIVEN

Say out Loud: I AM DRIVEN

Write It:

I AM DRIVEN

DAY 13

YOU ARE HUMBLE

Say out Loud: <u>I AM HUMBLE</u>

Write It:

I AM HUMBLE

DAY 14

YOU ARE WORTHY

Say out Loud: <u>I AM WORTHY</u>

Write It:

I AM WORTHY

DAY 15

YOU ARE FEARLESS

Say out Loud: I AM FEARLESS

Write It:

I AM FEARLESS

DAY 16

YOU ARE A LEADER

Say out Loud: <u>I AM A LEADER</u>

Write It:

<u>I AM A LEADER</u>

DAY 17

YOU ARE  BRILLIANT

Say out Loud: <u>I AM BRILLIANT</u>

Write It:

I AM BRILLIANT

DAY 18

YOU ARE SMART

Say out Loud: <u>I AM SMART</u>

Write It:

<u>I AM SMART</u>

DAY 19

YOU ARE ROYAL

Say out Loud: I AM ROYAL

Write It:

I AM ROYAL

DAY 20

YOU ARE LOVED

Say out Loud: <u>I AM LOVED</u>

Write It:

<u>I AM LOVED</u>

DAY 21

YOU ARE A WORLD CHANGER

Say out Loud: <u>I AM A WORLD CHANGER</u>

Write It:

<u>I AM A WORLD</u>

<u>CHANGER</u>

Conclusion

Understanding that it takes 21-days to form a habit, this book is done with our children in mind. I provide young readers with 21 powerful declarations to remind them of the excellent characteristics they possess.

Historically, during slavery, our ancestors purposefully did not speak well of us to protect us from being taken or violated by slave owners. * This generationally learned behavior must now be unlearned.

You Are is a step in that direction.

It is my sincere hope that we as adults will do our part to decrease and destroy "vacant esteem" in our children and even within ourselves.

I'm hopeful!

Be Blessed,
Cilvia Osborne

LET'S MAKE DECLARATIONS TOGETHER!

DeGruy, J. Post Traumatic Slave Syndrom America's Legacy of Enduring Injury and Healing. Portland OR: Uptone Press, 2.

Glossary

1. **Beautiful**– possessing qualities that give great pleasure or satisfaction to see, hear, think about, etc.; delighting the senses or mind
2. **Confident**: to be sure of oneself; having no uncertainty about one's own abilities
3. **Gifted**: having great special talent, ability or high intelligence
4. **Responsible**: involving accountability or responsibility, as in having the power to control or manage
5. **Courage**: the quality of mind or spirit that enables a person to face difficulty, danger, pain, etc., without fear; bravery
6. **Trustworthy**: deserving of trust or confidence; dependable; reliable
7. **Powerful**: having great power, authority, or influence; mighty; effectiveness
8. **Inspiring**: a divine influence directly and immediately exerted upon the mind or soul.
9. **Creative**: resulting from originality of thought, expression, etc.; imaginative:
10. **Amazing**: to overwhelm with surprise or sudden wonder; astonish greatly
11. **Loving**: feeling or showing love or great care
12. **Driven**: motivated or determined by a specified factor or feeling
13. **Humble**: not proud or arrogant; modest
14. **Worthy**: having adequate or great merit, character, or value
15. **Fearless**: bold; unafraid
16. **Leader**: a person or thing that leads
17. **Brilliant**: exceptionally clever or talented
18. **Smart**: clever, witty, or readily effective, as a speaker, speech, etc.
19. **Royal**: having the rank of a king or queen
20. **Loved**: held in deep affection; cherished
21. **World Changer**: a person who changes the world for the better

70342765R00027

Made in the USA
San Bernardino, CA
28 February 2018